Poetry from the Chambers of My Heart

Love and Pain

Martina E. Faulkner

Foreword by Taylor Wray

▌ INSPIREBYTES OMNI MEDIA

This publication is published and distributed worldwide in the English language in the following formats:

ISBN Paperback: 978-1-953445-65-0
ISBN Ebook: 978-1-953445-66-7

Library of Congress Control Number: 2024949668

This book was printed in a manner that minimizes its impact on the planet and the environment. Learn more at: www.inspirebytes.com

⧉ INSPIREBYTES OMNI MEDIA

Inspirebytes Omni Media LLC
PO Box 988
Wilmette, IL 60091

For more information, please visit www.inspirebytes.com
Cover artwork by Frances E. Vail

For those who choose love

Foreword

Vulnerability is both by necessity,
Strength and weakness.
My essence my protection, and yet
The bullseye on my back.

These lines from Martina Faulkner's "By Necessity
Always" perfectly capture the quality that immediately
struck me about this remarkable collection of poems:
Martina's bold display of vulnerability and the inspiring
strength intrinsic in that openness.

In *Love and Pain: Poetry from the Chambers of My Heart,*
Martina explores the dual themes of love and pain by
turning her poet's eye to what is, to use her phrase, both
unique and universal about our experiences of them.
Her introspective and at times painfully honest verse is
intensely personal, but ultimately profoundly familiar. In
Martina's poetry we find, with knowing recognition, that
love may be the passionate immediacy of surrendering one's
lips to another's, but also the simple, quotidian comfort
of a quiet "sleep well." Pain may be the sense of emptiness
in a bed that now feels too big, or a grieving plea to a loved
one who left this life too soon.

What I especially love about these poems is their full
and unflinching embrace of the knowledge that opening
our hearts to love also requires opening them to pain. In
these pages, Martina conveys—movingly, powerfully,
eloquently—the messy beauty of the way love and pain

are interlaced, and she shows us why poetry, perhaps more than any other art form, can perfectly capture the human heart's remarkable ability to hold both the exquisite highs of love and the crushing lows of pain at the same time.

Our experiences of love and pain and the relationship between them shape us as individuals and define us as human beings. It is my hope that you find in this book, as I have, a deeper appreciation of how that truth connects us, and comfort in the understanding that when we accept—and even embrace—love and pain as forever "intertwined bedmates," as Martina writes, we will always find the way forward.

Taylor Wray
October 2024

Introduction

I believe that poetry can take us on a journey from our minds to our hearts and souls in ways unavailable to other forms of the written word. Often poured forth by its creator, poetry captivates us in its exploration of the human condition. It captures and reflects a spectrum of human experience from both lived and witnessed perspectives.

There is no subject, however, that may be more explored and expressed in poetic form than love. Love is as unique and universal as being human and can be expressed in infinitely different ways from one person to another. Though the Greeks primarily identified four types of love (Storge, Philia, Eros, and Agape), it is clear that poetry represents infinitely more. The vast array of odes to love throughout the ages is testament to its importance in helping us understand what it means to be human—what it means to love.

Similarly, pain seems to be one of love's many companions. For where there is love, there is also potential for pain. In fact, the depth of the pain experienced at the end of love often reflects the magnitude of the feelings once shared. In this way, love and pain seem to have no limits.

There is nothing more palpable to the human heart than love and pain. Capturing just a glimpse of these experiences in words and phrases becomes an exercise in both vulnerability and strength. More so, perhaps, exploring these themes can serve as a reminder that pain is often always temporary and ever-changing in its intensity, while with love anything— including life, itself— feels infinitely possible.

Contents

By Necessity Always

I am simultaneously
as strong as a spider's silken thread
and as delicate as its web;

Able to sustain my own life, and yet
in need of protection;

Able to create pure beauty from air, and yet
weak to dismantling forces' attention.

Vulnerability is both by necessity,
strength and weakness.

My essence my protection, and yet
the bullseye on my back.

The Songwriter

Strumming your guitar,
Tho' I am so far away,
I can hear you in my head and heart
Every night and every day.

You said to find myself,
When I felt desperate to be seen.
You said I'd play again,
But I didn't know what that could mean.

There were days when your words
Repeatedly echoed in my head.
Just as there have been days when it was hard
To even get myself out of bed.

It's not fair! It's not right!
I screamed, *Why me?*
Then I turned on the soundtrack of your life
And allowed myself to be.

When you're dreaming in the studio,
Does your heart show you the way?
Did you know your words have power,
Creating gifts for strangers to play?

Oh my friend, you magical soul,
It seems there's so much you don't know,
About who you are, and why you're here,
And how you've helped me grow.

For now, let's leave it simply:
Please know you've done your part.
Your words, your voice, your music,
Have helped to heal my heart.

VIP Access

The access is flowing
Behind the VIP ropes
We live outside
The lines
When we are special
When others call us
Special.

No access is limited
Immortality is possible
Nothing is taken away
Always present
Always available

Until you're not
Until you're taken
Until you are no longer
Accessible
To me

Time is the great bouncer
Limiting our lives
To what we see
Before us
Even when we're
Walking blind

We don't see it
The access
We don't get it
The promise of tomorrow
Is as fleeting as the
Checklist in his hand

What if we could
Forever be VIPs
Forever know each other
Access each other

Remember
The bouncer is always
Looming
Let's make the most of life
Behind the velvet ropes
Before it's gone

Anti- Anti-Aging

Wrinkles and bumps and sometimes I'm crabby
Some skin is tight and some of it's flabby

Creams and potions
Movement and motions

All to change the march of time
All to feel that my life is still mine

Thirty-five instead of fifty plus
But who's really forcing us?

To live as if we haven't lived
And believe that age without aging is a gift?

Finally, it made sense when I changed perspective
When I looked at life with a new directive:

To live fully, without fear or even apology,
Embracing all that life is and has to offer me.

In this moment, choosing that which makes me feel my best
Including the lotions, the motions, and the rest.

The filter is no longer anti-aging;
It's changed by choice to life-engaging.

A Gentle Deepness

As you held me close in your arms
I felt my heart in my chest.
It was flipping over on itself;
How was I ever to get some rest?

You offered me the sweetest of kisses
As you said good night and sweet dreams,
Which caused my mind to envision
Stardust trails amid rivers of moonbeams.

How you have chosen to love me,
With a gentle deepness of embrace,
Is nothing I ever knew before,
Making me feel seen, loved, and safe.

My lips are now yours
As you tenderly touch my chin,
Making me long to feel you beside me,
Touching me, skin to skin.

There is no "sweet dream" that compares
No "good night" my mind can create,
That makes me feel better than I feel right now
Wrapped up in love, in your arms' embrace.

Glastonbury

Our story isn't over,
It's only our first song that has played.
Because we are a festival, not a radio,
And we still have many more days.

Even though leaving would be easier
Even though ending might seem smart,
It's learning how to stay together
That is the true gift of the heart.

Come Back to Me

I wish you could stand on the stool
And sing for me one more time,
Because when I hear your sweet voice echoing
The melody makes my heart cry.

Like bouquets of love in a vase
With their heady aroma filling the room with song,
My tears of joy and happiness hold me
Then tell me that you're not really gone.

It may seem simple, but it's these moments
That tell me everything will be alright,
Especially when everything feels heavy and scary
Or darker than the deepest night.

It's your voice, your tune, and your smile,
They are everything I need and adore,
And even when you are gone from me tomorrow
They will bring you back to me once more.

It's Better

Nights without you
aren't the same
Now that I don't hear your voice
Saying my name

No giggles
No chats
No wiles

No hugs
No hands
No smiles

The bed is larger
And the covers are all mine
But the clock ticks louder
As it keeps track of time

No love
No depth
No connection

No touches
No kisses
No affection

Time passing makes it easier
As I think of what we once had
From the initial dates and laughter
To the endless sadness and being mad

In the end, it's better
because now there are
No sighs and
No more lies

If I Could

If I could be me
In a world full of yous
Oh, just imagine, the wonderful things
I could do!

If I could fly
Instead of just run
Oh, just imagine, how much things
Could be fun!

If I could jump higher
Than the highest bright star
Oh, just imagine, how brightly
I could go far!

If I could share smiles
With everyone I meet
Oh, just imagine, how life
Could be sweet!

Now, If I could be ME
And if you could be YOU
Oh, just imagine, how amazing
The world would be too!

In Your Heart

Laughing and joking
as we giggle side by side
Hugging and nodding
when one of us has cried

Friends and lovers
we know what's true
You are there for me
as I am there for you

Always, together
even when we're apart
That's the simple truth of
someone who lives in your heart

Disavowed

I did my best to love you
I opened my heart
Exposed my wounds
You said the damage didn't scare you
You said you'd never leave
You said

Then you found logic
And the damage became
More than you realized
It was an excuse
For your fear
Your own story

And still I sleep alone

Best friends are rocks
You said you were a boulder
You said you knew
You said you loved me
You said

A pebble in a shoe can feel like a boulder
It's still a pebble
You thought you knew
You didn't understand
If you did, you wouldn't have walked away
You would have been that rock
Instead of the pebble

It doesn't matter
It wasn't meant to be
Even if it was
Ending your days with me
Looks quite different now

I wonder if you know what you meant
When you spoke from your heart
Before logic and fear stole the microphone

I wonder

It doesn't matter
I wish you well
I wish you joy
I wish you love

You may never know how you broke me
You said you're not a destroyer of lives
You said you couldn't hurt someone
You said

But you did
Not destroyed though
You didn't have that power
Only Changed
And hurt

And still I wish you well
Discernment will be my teacher now
Gone are the days of opening boxes together
Finding surprises
Sharing joys

Gone are the moments of connection
When I can smell the smoke and taste the bacon
Gone are the embraces, the knowing and the trust
Gone are the days of long talks and understanding
Gone are the nights of laughter and tears

In their wake only a wish
That you be well
And a prayer

That you are the last in the line
Of deceivers, impostors, and thieves
The original words you disavowed
And ended up embodying

Gone
Gone
Gone

Goodbye goofy,
I enjoyed kumquats for a while
And have lost my Lord protector
And
It seems
A friend

So be it and
I wish you well

How?

How do you
Say
Goodbye
To
Someone you
Didn't have
Enough
Hellos
With?

How do you
Wake
When sleep
Is
Absent
So there's nothing
To wake to?

How do you
Stand
When falling
Is more like
Breaking
Open
And the pieces
Scatter
Everywhere?

How is life
Lived through
Pain and love
Love and pain
When
Everyday
Is lived in both
Moments?

From January to December

Be strong when I'm weak
Be gentle when I'm feeling tattered
Hold me when I can't seem to hold on to anything and
Help me pick up the pieces when I've left them all scattered

Follow the power of the ocean and
Be my anchor when I can't sail
Against the power of the wind
When I fear I might fail

There's a balance of nature in harmony
That we can draw on to stand
Knowing that when life feels hard
We need to only reach for each other's hand

Your hand in mine, and mine in yours
Is all we need to remember
Across rooms, across tables, across chairs
From January to December

"Sleep Well"

It's the simple things
Always the simplest things
That dent our hearts
Leaving forever impressions
On our souls

A "Sleep well"
Or making a cup of tea
A kiss on the forehead

Dew on a blade of grass
A morning song of a birds' choir
The distant rumble of thunder

Holding hands
Reaching out
Sharing a hot bath or
A glance or a smile
Across the room

It's in the knowing
The seeing
The honoring of
The simplest things
That make this life

Raucously Quiet

It's a quiet love
One of wind chimes
And puffy clouds

Unsettling from what came before
The noisy carnival of lights
A love full of flash and thrills

A love that was new and
Knew history
Banging away like cymbals in the marching band

Loud and boisterous
Immediate and urgent
Filled with passion and flame

Softer now the flames are embers
Hot coals waiting to be stirred
To be lifted and fanned

A quiet love
One of gentle acceptance
In honest farewells each time we say goodbye

From building skyscrapers
To excavating foundations
Bricklaying was never so rewarding, exhausting, confusing

Dreams find their place to start
In limitless exciting potential
Nurtured in concrete

It's a quiet love
With a raucous beginning
And a rousing finale

Yet to be played

Belief

I believe in the power of
chocolate and stars.

I believe in love and rainbows,
and getting hurt,
and belly laughs.

I believe in yes
and no,
and sometimes, maybe.

I believe that belief is greater
than reality,
both to our detriment
and our salvation.

Two Chambers

There are two
Always two
Pain and Love are bedfellows
Sharing an invisible wall
Keeping them separate
And joined
In our hearts
Forever

Forever.

Forever the intertwined
Bedmates will breathe into life
Over morning tea
And afternoons in the sun

How grateful to have lived
This life with these bedfellows
Guiding me forward
Guiding us forward
Into the tomorrows we
Expected but never wanted

It's Just Pain

Everything in me hurts right now.
That despondent hurt.
The kind that's dull,
Chronic, and
Unidentifiable.

Pain.

It's just pain.

And pain passes.
And will come again.
And pass once more.

A Different Place

He was a twinkling star
trying desperately to shine
in a darkened sky.

Lighter than night
but darker than day
I watched him try to fly.

His wings were clipped
or at least he believed
they were too weak,

As every time he tried to take off
he became even too afraid
to even speak.

There was nothing I could do
but stand by his side
in the quiet space,

Where friends sometimes become lovers
and sometimes realize that gift
is best found in a different place.

What If

What if I gave thanks every day of the year
What if I gave thanks for things I didn't want to hear

What if I gave thanks for things that hurt me
What if I gave thanks for things I couldn't see

What if I gave thanks even when I didn't know
What if I gave thanks even after I take a blow

What if I gave thanks before I was blessed
What if I gave thanks when I felt a mess

What if I gave thanks with no expectation
What if I gave thanks in every situation

What if I gave thanks for the littlest of things
What if I gave thanks when I felt tangled in strings

What if thanks is the key
To feeling more like me
To moving through the pain
And returning to love's refrain

Would I Be

Would I be happier if

My wallet were thicker
and
My waist were thinner

My patience were longer
and
My frustrations shorter

My friends were nearer
and
My woes further

My hobby-time bigger
and
My to-do list smaller

Would I be happier if you loved me more
or
If I loved you less

Sighs and Gasps

How many days
How many nights
Will I
Still sigh?

Breath comes in doses
But not often enough
Sometimes I find myself
Catching
Gasping
Sucking air out of the world around me
Wide-mouthed
Like a fish on a line
Out of water
Desperate to keep living.

Living
Even though it feels more often
Like leaving
Is the solution
The only answer to the pain
The only idea that makes it
Go away.

It doesn't
It never will
Nothing can remove the hurt
Because then it would also remove
The love.

The love created the home
The love created the space
In which I called you mine
In my heart
Losing you put pain in the love
Losing the pain means
Losing the love.

And still I gasp
And sigh.

Like clockwork
To set a watch to
But who wears watches anymore
Like them
You are gone, too.

And it hurts.
And the pain remains
With the love.

Arms

Being with you reminds
Me how lonely I am
Lovely I am
Loving I am

Being apart I find
False strength shrouded
In motivation
Determination
Courage

Because there's nothing else to do
But move continuously forward

Is it false?
It feels it
Sometimes

Being with you I am bold
And free
And safe

Is safe freeing?
Or a cage?
A cage of comfort
Or a strong tailwind setting me
On my journey

How do I measure whether I am
Emboldened or withheld by your arms?
Loved or caged?
Supported or suppressed?

You see a side of me
Nobody
Knows
And yet

And yet

And yet

There's always more
Always a promise that was never a promise
Even though it was

Do your arms hold me up when I fall
Or help to keep me from flying?

How will I know?
I don't know

What is Love, then?
A promise?
A hope?

An embrace?
What if Love is nothing
And everything
All at once

I'm left questioning once again
Even though I know
Somewhere
I know

Loving
Lovely
Loneliness
Is all
Love

In its time.

The Hardest Part

I listened to the night come to life
all around me
as I sat on a limestone and granite chaise
inside a cauldron
of stone.

I am a lighthouse
a stone cairn
in the wilderness.

The hardest part
of creating
is patience.

I'm Just Me

I'm just me and that's all I can be.
You're just you and that's all you can be too.
And it's more than okay
For us to be that way,
Because we don't need to be other stuff
To make us enough.

We don't need the praise, the things, and the approval.
In fact, too much of that stuff is cause for our removal
From who we are inside, what we know to be true,
Like when you look at me, or I look at you.

When we look in the mirror, too often we stare with fury.
We don't see the love, the joy, and the beauty.
We stress over what we are not, or wished that we were,
Like him, or them, or anybody—especially her!

We notice the hurt, the pain, and the flaws.
We only see blemishes, while craving applause.
We want what we think will bring peace to our hearts.
We search for the answers in everything that keeps us apart.

Apart from ourselves, apart from each other,
Forever in competition, one always better than another.
There is no judgment, no comparison to be made,
Because we are all perfect—inside and out—in our own ways.

So, you just do you, and I'll just do me,
And together we'll make this world
A better place to be.

Ethereal Flower

You are like an untamed flower
Ethereal in your beauty
Captivating
And yet
Wild in your nature
My life changed the day I met you
The universe in a drop
The sky in a petal
The earth in a glance

My breath falters
Yet my lungs fill
Ready
Hungry
Eager for more
Of your nature, of you
Breathing you in
Holding you close
I'm captivated
By your presence
By your heart
By you

To Henry

As I lay a stone on your hearth
Crossing your invisible threshold
To the place where you found
Truth.

My friend, may I continue your legacy
The legacy of all
Who saw Truth
And found courage
Enough
To write.

So I say
Good day to the night.
And
Good night to the day.

Wind on the Grass

I am two people
The one you see
And the one you think
You can see
But never know.

Just because pain isn't a lipstick
Doesn't mean I don't wear makeup.

Have you ever watched the wind
Roll across the grass
At eye level?

I don't want to die
Without having
Fully lived.

We Watched

Neither of the earth
Nor of the skies
My life seems lived
Through different eyes

The air smelled of old wood
Musty with a hint of leather
As it lingered in the air
And we watched the changing weather

I have been neither
And both at the same time
In your arms
I finally felt like I could be mine.

A Prayer of Gratitude

Thank you for the stars
that shine in the night.

Thank you for the dark
and thank you for the light.

Thank you for the love
and hope in my heart.

Thank you for the beauty of
music, words, and art.

Thank you for nature
that surrounds me every day.

And thank you for the gifts
that are already on their way.

The Bee's Back

I got to stroke the back of a bumble bee
And sit in the shade of an old maple tree

While watching the clouds drift by overhead
And making the grass a comfortable bed

The birds flew by darting this way and that
And I watched a dragonfly make a home on my hat

Life slows down when you choose to make it
Just as it can speed up when you try to fake it

The fuzzy bee's back was a reminder to make the choice
To sit back for a while, and listen to my own voice

I'm here, in this moment, ready to just be
So, take a breath, sit down, and listen with me

There's nothing we need to do right now so please take a rest
And enjoy the world around you; it's really what's best

Infinite In My Heart

Broken-hearted is a lie
For you can't break a place
Where you reside

You never left my heart
Though you left my body
You were there before time began
And there you will remain

You grew its walls
Expanded its depths
And nurtured its breath

Though you have stepped away
From my being
You are always with my soul
Residing in my heart

As you should be
As I am in yours

This is the truth of love
Love that never breaks
Only takes different forms
Throughout different times

A love that transcends
Our very existence
And our daily presence
Survives unbroken

I Wish...

I wish you the
flexibility,
curiosity, and
determination
of a cat
who has just
found
an empty box.

A Wedding Poem

Hand in hand
They walked
Across miles
Along rivers
Down paths
That led them home

Smile to smile
They laughed
Sharing joy
Sharing stories
Sharing rest
That led them home

Heart to heart
They danced
Never doubting
Always listening
And returning
To the music
That led them home

Soul to soul
They remembered
What it was
To live
To breathe
To love
To believe

And it led them
To each other, to home

It led them
To a promise
To choose
To hold
To share

A promise to wake
To choose
To hold
To rest
In each others' arms,
Home.

Standing To Go Home

How can I stand in my boots
When my muscles are fatigued and
My tendons are worn and tattered?

When the bones of my frame
Are collapsing in on each other
And time won't pause for restoration?

How can I claim my space
When simply standing
Has become intolerable?

And the only strength came from hope.
Hope as multi-vitamin and steroid
Hope as prayer and belief

That someday, one day, strength would return
And my muscles and tendons would move my frame
With ease and flexibility.

That hope would lead to freedom,
And that freedom would lead to...
Peace.

A haven.

Where standing and flying are one,
And everything grows in possibility,
Watered by love, and
Sound in the knowing.

A haven where there is only
The steady flow of movement,
Wrapped in the guise
Of creativity.

Of joy.
Of love.
Of intimacy.
Of words.
Of comfort.
Of laughter.
Of smiles.
Of hands, touching.

Of... home.

Then, at last
Standing on a square foot,
Solidly in my boots,
I will be ready
To go home.

We will be ready
To go home
Together.

Onward

Footprints in meadows
Guide us
Forward toward
A life unimagined
Or caution us to
Turn back
Choose another way

There is no fork
Only blank canvas grasses
Beckoning us

Onward

Shackled in Silence

I would be sad if you were gone;
But I'm sad every day I see you.

Stuck in a chair
Trapped inside a body
That doesn't work
Without giving up.

Your keen mind
Shackled in silence,
By silence.
The loudest sound
I've known.

Maybe the flu means freedom
Maybe it just means rest.
Either way,
I'm still sad.

Sparking Stars

The wind was very hot and the sun burned bright
Yet still all the days were as dark as the night

With no room to breathe, and no end in sight
The firebeaters fought each flame with all of their might

It was the worst the modern world had known
Of rivers of fire, and ash, and smoke

I know it hurts you, but please don't cry,
For now there are half a billion more angels in the sky

One More Day

I wish I had
one more day
with you.
With us.
Then everyday
I'd wish again,
and again,
until
one more day
became
a lifetime of days
stretching
to the end
of time.

Simple

There are days when
My heart hurts
From missing you.

There are nights when
My brain screams
From not hearing you.

There are breaths when
My soul trembles
From losing you.

And there are lifetimes when
I know
I will see you again.

When We Gather

When we gather
We will hug longer
More often

We will smile more
At the little things
That give us pause

We will hold on tighter
Not for fear of losing
But for the love of having
Each other

When we gather
We will remember
That it's not in what we want
That we are made whole
But in caring for what we need

Connection
Community
Hope
Laughter
Touch
Breath
And Presence

Presence with each other
And the joy that comes in
Gathering.

How do I rise?

How do I rise?
Withered
Broken
Shriveled
Bent
With creaking limbs
And weakened strength,
I rise.
In inches
In seconds
In moments
Of doubt and fear
Buoyed by hope
And longing.

How do I rise?
Beaten
Defeated
Alone
Scarred and burned
On ungoverned flesh
Pushing
Lifting
Weighing
I rise.
In doubt
In hope
In love

Wrapped in flames
And knowing
Surrounded by ash.

How do I rise?
From emptiness
That has no end
Expansive
Ceaseless
Opened
With outstretched fingertips
Rays of possibility
Rooted in peat
And granite
I rise.
Believing
And holding
Being more
And nothing
Without ceremony
But to receptive
Arms.

I may fall, but
I will always
Rise.

Dear 2023...

I do not pretend to understand
all that you laid at my feet.
It was, at times, insurmountable
the mountains of loss and grief.

You also gave me many challenges
that were beyond difficult to bear.
Not because of the hurdles,
but because of how they made me aware.

Life, it seems, keeps going though,
no matter what is thrown our way.
And so with that I say, "Welcome 2024!"
For tomorrow is more than a brand new day.

Dear Andy

How much pain is one heart
supposed to endure,
can
endure,
before it breaks
into a billion tiny pieces?

Your leaving tested the limits
of my heart of tempered glass,
pushed it beyond breaking
to where it no longer
felt
shatterproof.

It simply lay down
in surrender
to the pain
like molten glass
fresh from the kiln
flopped
liquid
and untouchable
by bare hands.

We knew surrender
in ways others
couldn't
touch.

You were not supposed to go.
I told you you had more time
though I secretly knew you didn't.
It was too soon,
and yet
it always would have been.

I told you you had to wait
like the others
to see what came next.
I cherished your voice
and thoughts,
your words
and
your love.

Your faith and friendship
gave me a home
when words were
all
I
had.

You were not supposed to leave
before I hit my mark on the floor—
a little piece of tape that is supposed to
make everything make sense
or at least stable.
A place to stand.

I forgot to call;
I thought I had more time.
Tomorrow, I said,
twice.
But you left instead
without warning
without fanfare or ceremony
without suffering or pain,
at least in that
I am grateful.

What Life Scars

What is this thing we are doing
This thing we call life

Unlike the battle-worn soldier
I wear my scars on the inside
Where I can see them when I close my eyes
And they become most visible
When the world outside is darkened
And quiet

Life, like scars, has a way of showing up
Where it was previously unseen
A way of becoming so engrained
So much part of something
That they become invisible again

Like the fabric of life
These scars hold memories woven over time
Unlike life, the fabric of scars
Has no runs or tears in it
It grows more impermeable with time
More permanent
More indelible

As if they were tattooed in the ethers
These forever reminders
Become somehow inescapable

Enough

Violence begets violence
Fear begets fear
Hate begets hate
Until one day
The day
Someone says

Enough.

Enough with your words
Your actions and deeds
Enough with your smirks
Your smiles and needs
Enough with all that has kept me
Caged outside of myself
Enough with the pain
Enough with being stuck on a shelf

Enough.

When the violence
Ends
When the fear
Ceases
When the hatred
Ebbs
Is when I will know
It's been

Enough.

Journeying

See then, until the end,
where the struggle is.
And go there,
without prejudice ...
without pride ...

Auntie Jane knew
the boulders on the path
would always add
and help
even when there seemed
no way around
or through.

The end is the prize
but the reward is found
in the earning,
and the yearning.
When you touch me
with a glance
a single brush of
your fingertips
on mine.

We've won.

The Loving Thing *(For Jerry)*

When I reached out to you in tears
Not sure of what to do
You answered my call with love,
Listened, and offered a simple truth:

There is no right, and there is no wrong
There is only one thing that's true.
The answer you seek is inside your heart
Focus on love; it's all we're asked to do.

When you were diagnosed,
And long before you left,
I reached out to tell you another truth:
Your words were the greatest gift.

Be Difficult to Love

My darling girl
Be difficult to love
Be the fullness of who you are
Be the raw unbridled version of you
Be the soft, quiet heart
Be bold, be loud and free
Be pensive and hold onto hope
The hope for a love that transcends
Any difficulty
Any fear
Anything that makes you feel like
You need to change you
To be loved

You are loved.
You can be loved.

In your fullness
In your softness
In your boldness
In all that you are

You are loved.
You can be loved.

Love your strength
Your courage
Your passion
Your unyielding desire
Your belief
That anything is possible.

Love yourself for all of who you are
Because you can be loved
You are always loved

You are and always will be lovable
As you are
As you have always been
Even when others tried to make you
Believe otherwise

You are loved
You will always be loved
The ones who love you
Will love you – as you

Be difficult to love
So that it's easy for them
To find you
And love you.

The Evidence

I paint the sky
In clouds and
Swathes of blue
Filling the air
With every puff
Every wisp
Before I wipe
My slate clean
Droplets on the screen
The only evidence
That there was once
Something else

What I Know

My heart knows the honesty
of what it truly needs
Just as my soul knows the depth
of what it feels and sees.
All the while, my body longs
for the tenderness of your touch,
But my mind—my mind is finding this journey
to be almost too much.

Early on, you used the words
I deeply needed to hear
You offered me freedom to be,
to see, and to feel without fear.
I felt the rise of anticipation
send waves through my core
As I imagined what it would be like
to temporarily be yours.

As your lips find their way
to the back of my neck,
I feel your hands slide down my shoulders
to caress my breasts.
Gently following your lead,
I allow myself to give in
To the pleasure you offer,
to the way you touch my skin.

You say we can ride the currents
slowly and adeptly, together.
And yet, I hope you will provide me
with some sort of tether;
Because I know my heart,
my body, and my soul,
But my mind—my mind is afraid
of losing control.

You say you know, you think,
what I need to explore:
To be bold, to be free,
to be everything I am and more.
Tucked away from the world,
a safe space to let my mind go,
As my body and soul show up,
and I finally get to know:

What it feels to be fully present,
embodied and free,
What it feels to show up
as the fullest expression of me.
Without narratives, apologies,
agendas, or masks,
This is what you have offered,
this is what you have asked.

My heart knows this mini-journey
is designed for the best,
Even though my mind is continually
offering a second guess.
Both have given deference
to my body and soul,
The real leads in this play,
the ones with primary roles.

Can we be together and each find
our ways back to what's true?
What if we held space for it to happen,
to feel renewed?
Because I wish for you
to also find what you need
For you to find what you're seeking,
when you're with me.

Then we will know we have done our best,
done what we both needed to do
To honor our souls, our bodies,
our journeys, and our truths.
My only wish is simple: May we find the courage
to let go and just be
When I am with you,
and you are with me.

A Heart Not Likely Touched

I know this journey, this detour,
This pain.
It's reflected in a million songs
And their heartbreaking refrains

To wish upon a star
Upon another's heart
Is to place your hope in something
That could maybe fall apart

Plato's courage as salvation
Is something I need to embrace
Before I run out of time
Before I lose this race

If it's the promise of freedom
That I most long for,
Why does the fear of the unknown
Keep me from opening the door?

Be bold, embodied, open-hearted,
Be yourself, be free.
But conceal those parts that are just yours
Not meant for others to see.

Do you see me? The real me?
You think you do.
But I don't share it with many, as it's meant
Only for one, perhaps a few.

My heart is not likely yours, not here
To be touched by your dreams.
That's okay, I understand it's not about that,
Not this time, it seems.

This time it's about something else,
Something more, something we both need
To remember, to embody, to learn,
It's something to heed.

I give in to the journey, the higher plan
That's currently at play
Because I know in my heart, once I do,
The boulders will fall away.

Boulders that have kept me from the fullness
Of who I am—who I'm meant to be.
Weighted obstacles on my life's journey,
Constantly challenging me to be free.

And it's okay if you step away, unsure of
What this all means
It's a lot to take in, to embrace, as things
Aren't always what they seem.

I will still move forward on my heart's journey,
I will still prevail.
Because I don't have room to cower,
To doubt or to fail.

My heart belongs to another, as it has all along.
Even though we haven't found each other yet,
Because I haven't been ready, I haven't learned
What's truly needed to take that step.

And that's what you're offering,
If you still are,
To claim who I am, to walk freely
Through that door.

Then our karma will be complete,
Our journeys can parallel and continue,
And we can both be who we are
With the peace that comes from Truth.

Painting Words

You play with words
Like a master painter
Creating entire worlds
Out of letters and pauses
Deliberate
Mischievous
Playful
A craftsman at his craft
Plying and simultaneously
Prying me open
Open to your touch
Your mastery
Your desires
Especially as they meet mine
The mental foreplay
Is excruciating
In the best ways

Something Else

Detached and unattached
Are not non-attachment
They are the trying
The yearning
The hoping
While promising in little lies
Being something other
For someone else
Instead of yourself

I chose non-attachment
As did you
For the freedom
For the truth
For the hope of having
Something that resides
Outside the confines
Of expectation

Something raw
Something real
Something limitless
Something unseen
Something else
If only for a moment
For a time
For us

The Way

The way forward
Is always the same
As the ways before

We come from a long line of
Wisdom seekers
Prophetesses
Masters
Stone-turners
Gods
Enlightened ones
Teachers
Sages
Truth tellers
Keepers of hope
Light workers
Way showers
Star gazers

Each in their own
On their own
Paving the way forward
On paths laid before
And before them
When they open their eyes
To see
The way

What is Love?

The Greeks had words
To encompass it all
But can love be
Encompassed
Defined
Limited
To words

Or is love more
More feeling
More action
More presence

What is love but a
Feeling of
Hope
Peace
Comfort
Safety

I had forgotten what
Safe felt like
I had glimpses
I had ideas
But I forgot
Or perhaps
I never knew
Not really

Then he died and suddenly
Or a few months later
I realized how unsafe
I had been
Felt
Living

I clawed my way back
To safety
To comfort
To peace
And surviving became living
On its way to thriving
Until the safety mat
Was ripped out beneath me
Until violent rhetoric was
Condoned
Validated
Sanctioned

Now it feels no longer safe
Again

After decades of
Living in fear
And only months of
Living with peace
The fear has clawed its way
Back to the forefront

Back to the space
Where everything once
Felt possible
But feels hidden again

What is love, then?
It is peace
It is hope
It is joy
It is possibility
And
It is feeling safe

Acknowledgments

To those who have taught me about love in all its forms...
To those whom I have loved and have yet to love...
To those who have helped me remember love...
To those who have loved me...
Love is a gift... Thank you.

A special thank you to Taylor Wray, one of my favorite poets, your thoughtful words and insightful comments in the Foreword bring a smile to my heart. Additionally, thank you to Katherine for your editing prowess.

Author's Note

Happiness is often associated with love, just as unhappiness is associated with pain. I have found, however, that one can feel happiness in the midst of unthinkable pain, and unhappiness while in love. Neither happiness nor unhappiness are permanent states of being. They are emotions, and like all emotions, they ebb and flow. The trick is in allowing them to move, without holding on too tightly or getting lost in the thoughts that materialize during the waxing and waning.

In the end, we are all shaped by the happiness and un-happiness—the love and pain—that we experience. I have found that expressing these events in poetic form has allowed me to move through the accompanying waves of emotion with more ease. While these poems reflect moments from my own life, they are not unique only to me, nor are they finite. I know that love and pain will continue to intertwine in my life and help me evolve in ways I've yet to discover... as I hope they will for you, too.

About The Author

Martina E. Faulkner is a cross-genre author whose work focuses primarily on exploring what it means to be human. Whether it's in poetry or prose, nonfiction or fiction, children's books or articles, she uses her craft as a writer to inspire and entertain. Ultimately, her hope is that her words will help make life a little better for her readers.

A self-proclaimed Anglophile, Martina drinks tea daily and loves to look at beautiful images from the British Isles while dreaming up her next book. This is Martina's second book of collected poems, delving into the very human experiences of love and pain.

You can find Martina's regular column—*Unique and Universal*—on Substack, join Martina on Instagram and Facebook (@martinaefaulkner), or learn more at: www.martinafaulkner.com

More by the Author

Infinite In My Heart
Poems of Love, Loss, and Hope

50 and F*ck It!
Learn How You Can Let Go, Stand In Your Boots, and Truly Live!

What if..?
How to Create the Life You Want Using the Power of Possibility

Me: 365
A 5-Year Question-A-Day Journal

The Author's Journey
Your Roadmap to Navigating and Understanding the Publishing Industry

Crafting the Perfect College Essay
Write Your Best Essay in 3 Easy Steps

Children's Books by Martina E. Faulkner as Tia Martina

When the World Went Quiet

Princess Wigglebottom and the Forgotten Christmas